2-01

Canada in the 21st Century

Dominion of Canada

Suzanne LeVert

George Sheppard
Upper Canada College
General Editor

CHELSEA HOUSE PUBLISHERS
Philadelphia

Opposite: A sidewalk café in Quebec

Chelsea House Publishers
EDITOR IN CHIEF: Stephen Reginald
MANAGING EDITOR: James D. Gallagher
PRODUCTION MANAGER: Pamela Loos
ART DIRECTOR: Sara Davis
DIRECTOR OF PHOTOGRAPHY: Judy Hasday
SENIOR PRODUCTION EDITOR: J. Christopher Higgins
ASSISTANT EDITOR: Anne Hill
PRODUCTION SERVICES: Pre-Press Company, Inc.
COVER DESIGNER/ILLUSTRATOR: Forman Group

First Printing
1 3 5 7 9 8 6 4 2

The Chelsea House World Wide Web address is http://www.chelseahouse.com

Library of Congress Cataloging-in-Publication Data
LeVert, Suzanne.
  Dominion of Canada / Suzanne LeVert; George Sheppard, general editor.
    p. cm.—(Canada in the 21st Century)
  Includes bibliographical references (p.) and index.
  ISBN 0-7910-6061-6
    1. Canada—Juveline literature. [1. Canada.] I. Sheppard, George. II. LeVert,
Suzanne. Let's discover Canada. Dominion of Canada. III. Title. IV. Series.
F1008.2 .L43 2000
971—dc21   00-034588

Contents

My Canada

by Pierre Berton

"Nobody knows my country," a great Canadian journalist, Bruce Hutchison, wrote almost half a century ago. It is still true. Most Americans, I think, see Canada as a pleasant vacationland and not much more. And yet we are the United States's greatest single commercial customer, and the United States is our largest customer.

Lacking a major movie industry, we have made no widescreen epics to chronicle our triumphs and our tragedies. But then there has been little blood in our colonial past—no revolutions, no civil war, not even a wild west. Yet our history is crammed with remarkable men and women. I am thinking of Joshua Slocum, the first man to sail alone around the world, and Robert Henderson, the prospector who helped start the Klondike gold rush. I am thinking of some of our famous artists and writers—comedian Dan Aykroyd, novelists Margaret Atwood and Robertson Davies, such popular performers as Michael J. Fox, Anne Murray, Gordon Lightfoot, k.d. lang, Céline Dion, and Shania Twain, and hockey greats from Maurice Richard to Gordie Howe to Wayne Gretzky.

The real shape of Canada explains why our greatest epic has been the building of the Pacific Railway to unite the nation from

A hiker explores the Tamarack Trail in Waterton Lakes National Park, Alberta.

sea to sea in 1885. On the map, the country looks square. But because the overwhelming majority of Canadians live within 100 miles (160 kilometers) of the U.S. border, in practical terms the nation is long and skinny. We are in fact an archipelago of population islands separated by implacable barriers—the angry ocean, three mountain walls, and the Canadian Shield, that vast desert of billion-year-old rock that sprawls over half the country, rich in mineral treasures, impossible for agriculture.

Canada's geography makes the country difficult to govern and explains our obsession with transportation and communication. The government has to be as involved in railways, airlines, and broadcasting networks as it is with social services such as universal medical care. Rugged individualism is not a Canadian quality. Given the environment, people long ago learned to work together for security.

It is ironic that the very bulwarks that separate us—the chiseled peaks of the Selkirk Mountains, the gnarled scarps north of Lake Superior, the ice-choked waters of the Northumberland Strait —should also be among our greatest attractions for tourists and artists. But if that is the paradox of Canada, it is also the glory.

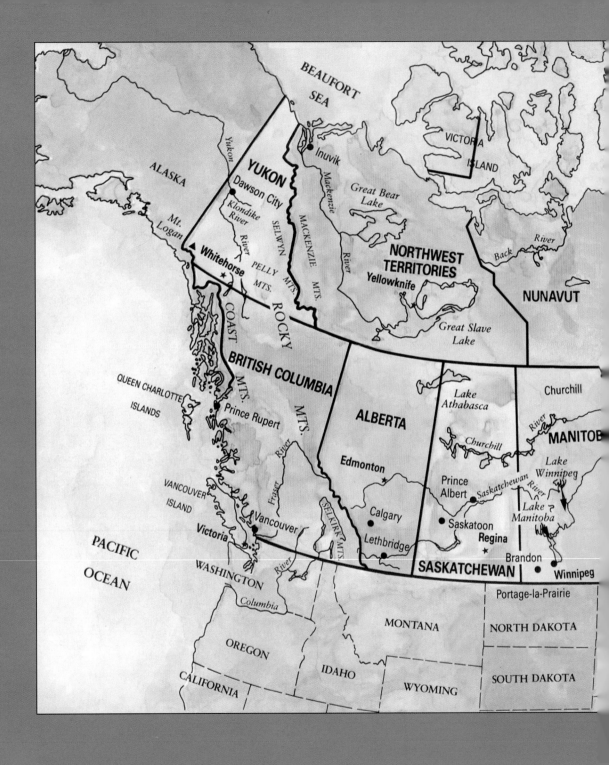

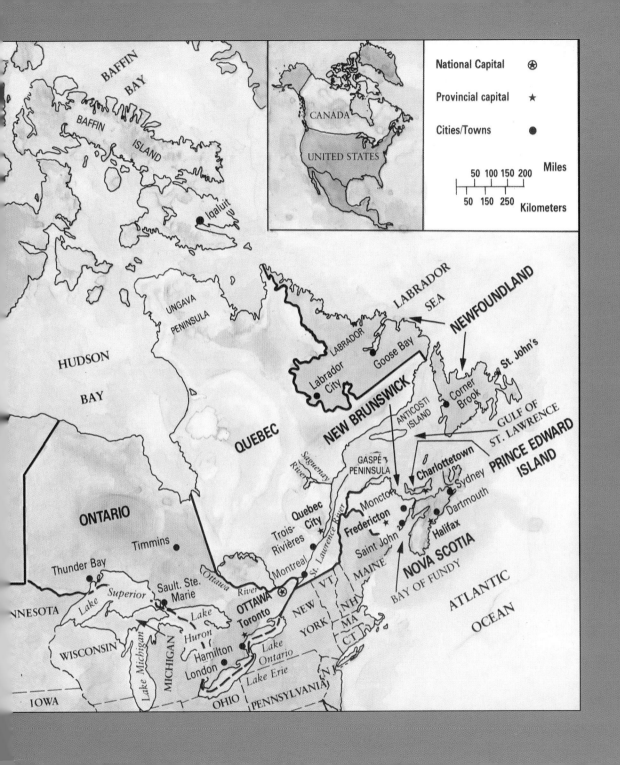

National Capital ⊗
Provincial capital ★
Cities/Towns ●

CANADA

UNITED STATES

Miles
50 100 150 200

50 150 250
Kilometers

BAFFIN
BAY

BAFFIN
ISLAND

Iqaluit

HUDSON

BAY

UNGAVA
PENINSULA

LABRADOR
SEA

NEWFOUNDLAND

LABRADOR

Goose Bay

Labrador
City

Corner
Brook

St. John's

QUEBEC

NEW BRUNSWICK

ANTICOSTI
ISLAND

GULF OF
ST. LAWRENCE

PRINCE EDWARD
ISLAND

Charlottetown

Sydney

ONTARIO

GASPÉ
PENINSULA

Saguenay
River

Quebec
City

Trois-
Rivières

Moncton

Fredericton

Dartmouth

Timmins

St. Lawrence River

Montreal

Saint John

Halifax

NOVA SCOTIA

Thunder Bay

Ottawa
River

MAINE

BAY OF FUNDY

ATLANTIC

OCEAN

Lake
Superior

Sault. Ste.
Marie

OTTAWA

NEW

VT

MINNESOTA

Lake
Huron

Lake Michigan

Toronto

YORK

NH

MA

WISCONSIN

MICHIGAN

Hamilton

Lake
Ontario

CT

London

Lake Erie

N

IOWA

OHIO

PENNSYLVANIA

Chronology

1000	Viking Leif Eriksson lands in Vinland, probably at the site now called L'Anse-aux-Meadows in Newfoundland.
1497	Navigator John Cabot explores Canada's east coast.
1534	Jacques Cartier explores the Gulf of St. Lawrence; landing on Quebec's Gaspé Peninsula, he claims the land for France.
1583	Humphrey Gilbert claims Newfoundland for Britain.
1608	French explorer Samuel de Champlain founds the city of Quebec.
1610	British explorer Henry Hudson discovers Hudson Bay.
1642	Ville-Marie de Montréal, later shortened to Montreal, is founded by French missionaries.
1670	A British trading firm called the Hudson's Bay Company is founded and given title to much of northern and central Canada.
1713	Under the Treaty of Utrecht, France surrenders to Britain its claims to Hudson Bay, Newfoundland, and most of eastern Canada.
1755	The British forcibly expel the Acadians (settlers of French descent) from Nova Scotia and New Brunswick.
1759	British forces under General James Wolfe defeat French troops on the Plains of Abraham outside Quebec City.
1763	The Treaty of Paris ends decades of fighting between the French and British in both Europe and Canada. France gives its North American territory (except the small islands of St. Pierre and Miquelon in the Gulf of St. Lawrence) to Britain.
1774	The Quebec Act gives French Canadians political rights and religious freedom under British rule.
1789	Explorer Alexander Mackenzie follows the Mackenzie River from central Canada to the Arctic coast.
1807	Explorers David Thompson and Simon Fraser travel through what is now British Columbia.

1812	During the War of 1812 between the United States and Britain, many battles are fought in British North America (Canada). The British, French Canadians, and Native Americans are allies against U.S. forces.
1837	Factions in Quebec and Ontario rebel against the colonial government; the rebellions are crushed, but a British investigation results in greater independence for the Canadian colonies.
1840	The Act of Union unites Canada West (Ontario) and Canada East (Quebec) into the province of Canada, with a new parliament.
1848	The provinces of Canada and Nova Scotia gain self-government.
1857	Queen Victoria names Bytown (now Ottawa) the capital of Canada.
1864	Colonial leaders meet at Charlottetown, Prince Edward Island, to discuss creating the nation of Canada.
1867	Nova Scotia, New Brunswick, Quebec, and Ontario unite in a confederation called the Dominion of Canada. Sir John A. Macdonald is named Canada's first prime minister.
1869	Canada buys the western lands from the Hudson's Bay Company. In Manitoba, Louis Riel leads an uprising of Métis (people of mixed French and Native descent) against British rule. The rebellion is quickly crushed.
1870	The province of Manitoba is made part of the Dominion of Canada; the Northwest Territories is established.
1871	The province of British Columbia is added to the Dominion of Canada.
1873	The province of Prince Edward Island is added to the Dominion of Canada.
1885	The last spike is driven in Canada's transcontinental railway. Louis Riel leads a Métis revolt in Saskatchewan; he is captured and executed.
1896	Gold is discovered near the Klondike River in the Yukon district of the North West Territories, spurring the Klondike gold rush.

1898	The Yukon is given territorial status.
1905	The provinces of Saskatchewan and Alberta are added to the Dominion of Canada.
1926	Britain's Balfour Declaration recognizes autonomy for former British colonies, including Canada.
1931	The Statute of Westminster gives Canada nearly complete independence from Great Britain.
1947	Oil is discovered at Leduc, Alberta; Canada's oil industry begins large-scale development.
1949	Newfoundland becomes Canada's 10th province. Canada, the United States, and 10 western European nations form the North Atlantic Treaty Organization (NATO).
1959	The St. Lawrence Seaway, a joint U.S.-Canadian project, opens, allowing oceangoing ships to reach the Great Lakes.
1962	The Trans-Canada Highway, the nation's first ocean-to-ocean automobile route, is completed.
1965	The National Health Plan is introduced.
1967	Canada hosts Expo 67, a world's fair, to celebrate its 100th anniversary.
1970	A separatist movement called the Front de Libération Québecois (FLQ) kidnaps and kills Pierre Laporte, Quebec's minister of labor; the government responds by declaring the War Measures Act and arresting 500 Quebec separatists.
1976	Montreal hosts the Summer Olympics. The Parti Québecois, which advocates independence for Quebec, wins a majority in the National Assembly.
1980	Three-fifths of the people of Quebec vote to remain in Canada.
1982	Canada adopts a new constitution that ends British control over constitutional amendments; a Charter of Rights and Freedoms is added.
1989	Canada and the United States enact a free-trade agreement that will eliminate all tariffs on goods transported between the two countries by 1998.

1990   The Meech Lake Accord, which would have given Quebec special status within the Dominion of Canada, fails to become law.

1991   Goods and Services Tax introduced by Conservative government of Brian Mulroney.

1992   The next attempt to modify the Constitution, the Charlottetown Accord, also fails to become law.

1994   New Liberal government of Jean Chretien agrees to North American Free Trade Agreement. NAFTA includes the U.S., Canada, and Mexico.

1995   In another attempt at independence, a measure to create a sovereign state of Quebec—separate from Canada—is narrowly defeated at the polls, 50.6 percent to 49.4 percent.

1999   The Canadian map is transformed by the creation of Nunavut, created from the Northwest Territories. The population is 85 percent Inuit.

2000   Nisga'a treaty sees major shift in way federal government

Provinces and Territories Ranked by Population and Area

	Population	Area		Population	Area
Alberta	4	7	Nunavut	13	11
British Columbia	3	4	Ontario	1	3
Manitoba	5	6	Prince Edward Island	10	13
New Brunswick	8	10	Quebec	2	2
Newfoundland	9	9	Saskatchewan	6	5
Northwest Territories	11	1	Yukon	12	8
Nova Scotia	7	12			

The Making of a Nation

When European explorers landed on Canadian shores in the 16th century, they found a land filled with possibilities for settlement and economic growth. They sent word home that Canada's waters teemed with fish and that its dense forests were rich in timber and fur-bearing animals. But none of the early explorers or settlers predicted that the vast wilderness they found would become a leading world power by the 20th century. Today, Canada is an independent nation of more than 30.5 million people. The gleaming skyscrapers of its major cities house some of the world's largest corporations, its forests provide 40 percent of the world's newsprint, and its prairie farms feed millions of people in dozens of countries. Its citizens have included some of the world's leading scientists, scholars, artists, diplomats, and athletes. Four centuries have transformed Canada from an untamed wilderness to a modern industrial state.

Long before the Europeans arrived in what is now Canada, many different Native peoples inhabited its shores, forests, prairies, and northern tundra. According to anthropologists, the first Canadians may have arrived from northeastern Asia as many

Opposite: L'Anse-aux-Meadows, at the northern tip of Newfoundland Island, is one of several Viking settlements that archaeologists have found along North America's Atlantic coast. The settlement dates from about A.D. 1000 and consists of several sod-roofed huts. *Above:* A portrait made in London in 1709 shows a chieftain of the Mohawk people, who live in Canada north of lakes Erie and Ontario.

This 1922 Hudson's Bay Company calendar featured a Native fur trapper and, in the background, the company's Fort Prince of Wales as it probably looked in the 1730s.

as 50,000 years ago. Over the centuries, these immigrants and their descendants spread out through the New World, forming many distinct cultures, each with its own language, customs, and ways of life.

Vikings from Scandinavia and Greenland fished and logged on Canada's east coast as early as A.D. 1000. But lasting European contact did not begin until the early 16th century, when Britain, France, and other nations began sending explorers to search for new sea routes westward across the Atlantic and, later, to survey the lands they found in North America.

Almost immediately, Britain and France began to fight for control of northern North America and its resources. Each sent thousands of colonists to these new territories; the descendants of these settlers live in Canada today. The struggle between France and Britain in the New World lasted more than 150 years and included 4 major wars and countless raids and skirmishes. It ended in 1763, when the British finally defeated the French. France surrendered almost all of its claims in North America to Britain under the Treaty of Paris.

The treaty gave Britain control of three regions covering much of present-day Canada: the enormous former French colony that is now called Quebec; an island fishing colony on the east coast called Newfoundland; and Prince Rupert's Land, a vast tract of wilderness stretching northwest of Quebec. At first, Britain concentrated on expanding the fur trade, its most profitable business in the New World. Since 1670, Prince Rupert's Land had belonged to an English fur-trading firm called the Hudson's Bay Company (HBC). Over several centuries, millions of dollars' worth of beaver, fox, marten, and mink pelts were sent to England by the HBC traders in Prince Rupert's Land.

The HBC did more than bolster the British economy. The company and its rival, a trading firm called the North West Company, were responsible for mapping most of central and western Canada; Alexander Mackenzie, exploring on behalf of the North West Company, was the first European to cross North America, reaching the Pacific Ocean in 1793. The fur-trading companies also played a big part in the settlement of the Canadian wilderness. As the fur trade moved into new territory, small settlements grew up around trading posts in the western prairies and along the northern rivers.

While the west and north were being opened to settlement, the population of the eastern colonies was increasing. In the late 18th century, more than 40,000 British colonists fled to Canada to escape the American Revolution in the south. These Loyalists—as American colonists who remained loyal to Britain were called—settled mostly in the established colonies of Quebec and Nova Scotia. In Quebec, French inhabitants greatly outnumbered the British arrivals, and many institutions, such as the French Catholic church and French civil law, were unfamiliar to them. The Loyalists demanded their own colonies. In 1784 the British Parliament created New Brunswick from part of Nova Scotia. In 1791 it divided Quebec into two colonies. Lower Canada (present-day Quebec) was predominantly French, and Upper Canada (present-day Ontario) was predominantly English. But this division did not end friction between French-speaking and English-speaking Canadians, which has continued to the present.

In 1841, the British combined Lower Canada and Upper Canada into a single colony called the Province of Canada. The

Newfoundlanders in traditional British redcoat uniforms take part in a historical festival on Signal Hill, St. John's. Eastern Canada was the scene of many battles between the British and the French during colonial days.

part that is now called Quebec was renamed Canada East; present-day Ontario became Canada West. On the coast, Nova Scotia, New Brunswick, Prince Edward Island, and Newfoundland made up Atlantic Canada. As most of these colonies' populations continued to grow, so did their desire for political power and independence. In 1848, Britain gave some powers of self-government to the Province of Canada and the Nova Scotia colony. But many colonists wanted still more independence. They began to talk of confederating—that is, uniting the various colonies into a single confederation, a new nation. At this time, the United States was gaining in size and military strength, and many Canadians were afraid that their southern neighbor would invade their territory. They felt that a confederation of all the colonies would be able to protect Canada from invasion.

Confederation

In 1867, the British Parliament passed the British North America Act (BNA), which united the Province of Canada and the Atlantic colonies of Nova Scotia and New Brunswick into a new nation called the Dominion of Canada. At the same time, the Province of Canada was divided into the present-day provinces of Quebec and Ontario.

Not all Canadians were enthusiastic about confederation. Many people in Nova Scotia, for instance, felt that the colony should try to strengthen its unique position as a center of trade and shipping on the Atlantic seaboard rather than join a confederation whose interests lay westward and inland, where new territories in the prairies and mountains were growing in importance. Some Nova Scotians felt that they had far more in common with Britain and with Newfoundland and Prince Edward Island—two colonies in Atlantic Canada that refused to join the confederation—than with Quebec and Ontario. Although Nova Scotia did join the confederation in 1867, the regional differences that were expressed then still affect relationships among the Canadian provinces today. The citizens and leaders of

Delegates from the colonies met at Charlottetown, Prince Edward Island, in 1864 to discuss forming a union. These statesmen are sometimes called the Fathers of Confederation. From their deliberations the new nation of Canada was born.

the Atlantic provinces often feel that they have little in common with Canadians who live in the prairie provinces or in the highly industrialized provinces of Quebec and Ontario. Competition and rivalry among the provinces or regions often overshadows commitment to the federal union.

As settlers entered the western and northern territories, new provinces were created and brought into the confederation. Manitoba joined in 1870, after a bitter fight between the new wave of English-speaking settlers and the Métis, people of mixed French and Native descent who had lived in the region for more than 100 years. In 1871, British Columbia, on the Pacific coast, agreed to join the confederation—but only after the Canadian government promised to build a railroad that would link the western region to the more populous east. In 1873, tiny Prince Edward Island, in debt and eager to have a railroad built by the federal government, joined the confederation. The provinces of Saskatchewan and Alberta, their populations swollen by hundreds of thousands of immigrants from all over the world, were created in 1905 from a larger region known as the North West Territories; what remained of this region was the present-day Northwest Territories, Nunavut, and Yukon Territory. Newfoundland was the last province to join the confederation, in 1949.

One of Canada's biggest challenges was overcoming the barriers of geography to forge the diverse provinces and territories into a single nation. Canada stretches for more than 3,233 miles (5,187 kilometers) from the rocky coast of Newfoundland in the east to British Columbia's Coast Mountains in the west. The eastern and western parts of the country were separated not only by distance but by immense mountain ranges. The first European travelers in Canada—fur traders, explorers, missionaries, and a few stalwart settlers—had relied on the rivers for transportation. But only when a transcontinental railway was complete could extensive settlement and internal commerce take place. The building of the railroad helped create a new national spirit, a sense of a unified Canadian nation.

The construction of the Canadian Pacific Railway began in the 1870s and was marked by many delays, some due to scandals over government corruption and mismanagement of funds, others due to the sheer technical difficulty of laying track over Canada's rugged terrain. Across the rock and muskeg of the east, across the seemingly endless central prairies, over the peaks and gorges of the towering Rocky Mountains, and then finally through the thick forests and coastal ranges of British Columbia, the track was laid by tens of thousands of workers at a cost of $100 million. The last spike was driven in at Craigellachie, British Columbia, on November 7, 1885.

As the railway proceeded west, new cities sprang up one after another along its path, forming links in a chain across the southern

The workers who built the railroad through rugged western Canada blasted tunnels through the mountain walls and built log trestles across deep gorges. Despite the dangers and the difficulties, the railroad was completed in 1885.

part of the country. Later, other railways and branch lines opened up new areas for settlement to the north and south. In the 20th century, a road system was built to complement the network of railway lines. The first road traffic to the far north began during World War II with the construction of the Alaska Highway, completed in 1945. The Trans-Canada Highway, opened in 1962, was the first major roadway to span the country.

Modern Canada

The British North America Act of 1867 gave Canada only limited powers of self-government. It stated that Canada's government must be based on the British parliamentary system, with a British governor-general presiding over an appointed Senate and an elected House of Commons. The monarch of England remained monarch of Canada, and Great Britain retained formal control of Canada's foreign affairs. Although independent in its internal affairs, the Dominion of Canada was still part of the British Empire. Control over foreign affairs did not come for more than 60 years.

In the decades that followed confederation, Canada steadily gained international prestige and power, and many Canadians began to demand greater participation in shaping foreign policy. In 1923, Canada signed its first independent treaty with another country: an agreement with the United States to regulate fishing in the Pacific Ocean. In 1931, the British Parliament passed the Statute of Westminster, which officially recognized Canada as an independent nation. During the years that followed, other ties, both ceremonial and political, were severed. In 1980, for example, Canada stopped using the British "God Save the Queen" as its national anthem. The only anthem now used is "O Canada."

The long, slow process of separation was continued in 1982, when Canada passed the Constitution Act, which eliminated the need for British approval of constitutional amendments. The act, including a new bill of rights called the Canadian Charter of Rights and Freedoms, replaced the British North America Act as the basis for Canadian statehood.

In the early 20th century, thousands of workers migrated into the prairie provinces to work in the grain harvests. Many of them remained, forming new communities in Manitoba, Saskatchewan, and Alberta.

In 1993 Jean Chretien was sworn in as Canada's prime minister, a post he has held through the end of the 20th century.

Although its identity as a sovereign state is now clearly defined, Canada's cultural identity—its national spirit—is harder to define. Author Margaret Atwood, one of Canada's most admired cultural figures, has said that "to live in Canada is to choose a violent duality," by which she means that Canadian society often seems pulled in opposing directions. Canadians are frequently torn between conflicting ideas about their country and its position in the world. For one thing, Canada has two levels of government, the provincial and the federal, that often compete for the people's loyalty. During much of its history, Canada was a group of loosely allied colonies or provinces ruled by Great Britain. Each developed its own government, economy, and way of life. A strong sense of provincial identity lingers today, and many Canadians consider themselves residents of their province first and of Canada second.

Another duality in Canadian life has its roots in the legacy of the colonial period. The long struggle for supremacy between the two colonizing nations, France and Britain, still dominates Canada's culture and politics. The French-speaking and English-speaking people of Canada sometimes regard themselves as members of two different countries—and the province of Quebec, home of more than 90 percent of Canada's French-speaking population, has threatened to separate from the rest of Canada if it is not officially recognized as a distinct society. Quebec's insistence on being granted special rights and privileges has angered many English-speaking Canadians as well as Native peoples. Another effort toward independence came again in 1995, in the form of a Quebec provincial referendum on sovereign nation status. The move was narrowly defeated, 50.6% to 49.4%.

A third duality involves Canada's relationship with the United States. Most Canadians have conflicting ideas about the United States, which is perhaps the biggest obstacle to the development of a national Canadian identity. Although many Canadians admire and enjoy the culture and dynamism of their southern neighbor, others resent its proximity, its economic and political dominance, and its overwhelming influence on the Canadian way of life.

Robert Thompson, the leader of Canada's Social Credit party, said in the 1960s, "The Americans are our best friends whether we like it or not."

In many ways, Canada has defined its own identity by contrasting itself with the United States. Canada's political and social life is quite different than that of the United States. One of the basic differences is the degree of government funding for and administration of social programs. Whereas the United States has long emphasized individual rights and self-sufficiency, Canada has emphasized sharing and a sense of community. This communal attitude is reflected in Canada's social programs, which are a strong unifying factor within the country, applying to all Canadians everywhere. In 1958, a national program for hospital care was introduced, followed 10 years later by public health insurance to meet the costs of physicians' services. Today, every Canadian is eligible for free and comprehensive medical care. In addition, federal, provincial, and local programs provide a high level of income security through pension plans, family allowances, and other measures.

The 1990s brought major changes to Canada. Two attempts to change the country's constitution by Brian Mulroney's Progressive Conservative government failed and a goods and services tax of 7% was introduced. These helped propel the Liberals to victory in 1993. But Jean Chretien did not eliminate the GST as promised and his government expanded the FTA to include Mexico in the 1994 North American Free Trade Agreement (NAFTA). Perhaps most significantly, a new territory was created. Nunavut, carved from the Northwest Territories, has a population that is 85% Inuit.

Canada and the World

In the winter of 1991, Canadian military troops were at war for the first time in nearly 40 years. More than 1,700 Canadian sailors, soldiers, and airmen served with the multinational force arrayed against Iraq in the Persian Gulf war. About two dozen Canadian CF-18 jet fighters provided defensive air cover for allied naval vessels, including several Canadian ships, in the Persian Gulf. This was one of several times in the 20th century when Canada has taken part in international conflicts.

Located near both the United States and Russia, heavily dependent upon world trade across both the Atlantic and Pacific oceans, and with close connections to both French-speaking and English-speaking communities in the developing world, Canada's role in foreign affairs is often a balancing act—the country often remains neutral in disputes among other nations. Compared with most European powers and the United States, Canada has had little experience in international politics. From the time of confederation in 1867 until 1931, Canadian foreign relations were handled through the British government.

Opposite: Canadian soldiers on duty in Saudi Arabia in 1991. Canada was part of the multinational force arrayed against Iraq in the Persian Gulf war.
Above: Britain's Prince Charles (C) waves as he and his sons Prince William (R) and Prince Harry ride the quad chair lift up Whistler Mountain during their spring break ski vacation, at Whistler, Canada, March 26, 1998.

This close alliance with Britain often increased the tension between French-speaking and English-speaking Canadians, especially in times of war.

During World War I (1914–18), more than 600,000 Canadians of both French and British descent volunteered to fight in Europe and elsewhere on the side of Britain and France. Only near the end of the war, when the number of casualties was high and the number of volunteers was low, was the question of forced enlistment, or the draft, raised. Although French Canadians strongly opposed a draft, Prime Minister Robert Borden managed to put the draft into effect, increasing resentment toward the English Canadian government on the part of French Canadians. More than 24,000 Canadians were drafted and sent to Europe before the end of the war.

World War I strengthened Canada's domestic economy and increased its prominence in world affairs. After the war, Canada was viewed by the rest of the world as an independent nation, and

World War II sea battles in the North Atlantic sometimes raged close to Canadian shores. This Allied vessel drops depth charges off the coast of Halifax, Nova Scotia.

this status was confirmed by the British Parliament in 1931 with the Statute of Westminster. In 1939, Canada entered World War II on the side of Britain, France, and other Allied nations against Germany and the Axis countries. Canadian soldiers and aircrew were dispatched to Britain and thousands of sailors fought for years against German submarines in the "Battle of the Atlantic." The Canadian armed forces first saw action in the Pacific in December 1941. Before the war ended in 1945, more than 700,000 Canadians had seen active service, and 42,000 had lost their lives in Europe, Asia, or Africa.

Canada emerged from World War II as a leading power, with economic and political interests around the world. Since then, Canada has signed more than 1,000 international agreements and treaties and joined more than 200 international organizations. Canada is represented in other countries by the Department of External Affairs, which advises the Canadian government on foreign policy, foreign trade, and international defense. Canada maintains more than 100 diplomatic posts in 79 countries and also has 12 permanent missions, or staffs, that are assigned to international organizations, including the European Community (EC), the United Nations Educational, Scientific and Cultural Organization (UNESCO), and the Organization of American States (OAS).

Two of the most important international organizations to which Canada belongs are the United Nations (UN) and the North Atlantic Treaty Organization (NATO). Canada was one of the 51 founding members of the United Nations in 1945, and from the start it has been among the UN's most determined and consistent supporters, contributing both money and manpower to UN efforts. During the Korean War (1950–53), more than 22,000 Canadian soldiers were part of the UN force that fought against North Korea's invasion of South Korea. In 1956, Canada was a member of the UN peacekeeping force sent to the Middle East after Britain, France, and Israel invaded Egypt. Lester B. Pearson, then Canada's minister of foreign affairs, was awarded the Nobel Peace Prize in 1957 for organizing the UN force, which

Health care workers prepare vaccinations at a camp in Ethiopia. Canada maintains ties to many developing nations through programs that provide health care, food, and other aid.

restored order to the troubled region. Canada's military personnel now serve with UN forces in the Balkans and in Cyprus, the Golan Heights between Syria and Israel, and other locations in the Middle East. Members of the Canadian armed forces also help monitor the terms of the 1979 peace treaty between Egypt and Israel through the UN's Multinational Force and Observers Organization.

In 1949, Canada became a founding member of the North Atlantic Treaty Organization, which was formed by Canada, the United States, and eight other nations to defend against a possible attack by the Soviet Union and its communist allies. Canada's NATO troops, based in Germany, include both a land division and an air force. Membership in NATO has always been controversial among Canadians, some of whom feel that the cost of maintaining troops in Europe is too great and that the money would be better spent on the defense of Canada's own borders—for example, on more ships to patrol the 200-mile (320-kilometer) offshore fishing limit that the country has declared in its coastal waters. Ships from other countries are not supposed to fish inside the limit, but they occasionally do so.

In addition to military alliances, Canada maintains trade relations with countries around the world. Its major trading partner is the United States; other important partners are Japan and the United Kingdom.

Canada also maintains strong ties to the developing nations of the world by donating various types of aid to more than 100 Third World countries. In 1988–89, Canada contributed more than $1.4 billion to programs designed to provide food, rural and agricultural projects, and technical assistance to these nations. Due to federal budget concerns, however, Canada's foreign aid expenditures were significantly reduced in the 1990s.

Canada and Its Southern Neighbor

Canada and the United States share the world's longest undefended border: 5,535 miles (8,900 kilometers). The two nations are also linked by an intricate network of laws, agreements, and arrangements that deal with military defense, the environment, fisheries, and energy. But because the United States has a much larger population, is considerably more aggressive in exporting its culture, and plays a larger role in international affairs, Canada often feels overwhelmed by its neighbor to the south.

Since the end of World War II, Canada and the United States have been close partners in the defense of North America. In 1958 the two nations established the North American Air Defense Command (NORAD) against the possibility of air attack by the Soviet Union. In 1985 they signed a renewed NORAD agreement that included plans to modernize and improve air defense capabilities.

Canada and the United States are each other's strongest trading partners. Trade with the United States accounts for 73 percent ($98 billion) of Canada's exports and 65 percent ($86 billion) of its imports. The United States, in turn, is deeply dependent on commerce with Canada: U.S. trade with the Province of Ontario alone exceeds U.S. trade with Japan.

In 1989, Canada and the United States signed a joint Free Trade Agreement (FTA), a bill that eliminated all tariffs (import duties) and other restrictions on trade between the 2 nations over a 10-year period. In 1994 Mexico joined this association through NAFTA. Some economists believe that the agreements will expand the volume of trade, increase employment, and raise incomes in both countries. Not all Canadians agree, however. Many feel that

Canada and the United States share the world's longest undefended border. That border runs down the middle of Niagara Falls, between New York State and Ontario, seen here from the Canadian side.

the agreements strongly favor the United States. Because taxes, property values, and production costs are generally lower in the United States than in Canada, many manufacturers and employers find it less expensive to operate there, and some Canadian businesses have moved to the United States or gone out of business entirely, costing Canadian workers their jobs. In addition, in the early 1990s it was often cheaper to buy some consumer goods in the United States than in Canada. Thousands of Canadians still cross the border to shop in the United States in order to pay lower prices and taxes, especially on goods like cigarettes and gasoline.

Trade is not the only controversial issue in U.S.-Canadian relations. Pollution control—specifically, the amount of acid rain that crosses the border in both directions—has become a pressing issue. According to environmental experts, Canada receives more than twice the amount of airborne pollutants from the United States that the United States gets from Canada. In 1990, U.S. President George Bush signed the Clean Air Act, which required that the United States reduce by half the amount of emissions that cause acid rain (primarily sulfur dioxide) by the year 2000. In 1991, Bush and Prime Minister Brian Mulroney of Canada signed the U.S.-Canada Agreement on Air Quality, which required that Canada also limit its sulfur dioxide emissions. While sulphur dioxide emissions were reduced, partly by requiring more stringent emissions standards for 1998 and newer cars, an estimated 50 to 80% of smog in Ontario and the Maritimes is still traced to U.S. sources.

Another issue confronting the two nations involves fishing rights in both the Atlantic and Pacific oceans. One particularly bitter dispute concerns the border that divides the lucrative Pacific salmon catch between Canada and the United States. Canada recognizes a 1903 boundary that crosses the southern tip of the Alaska Panhandle, giving Canada access to the Pacific along 25 miles (40 kilometers) of coastline that the United States says belongs to Alaska. Each nation has occasionally seized fishing vessels belonging to the other in these contested waters.

Although Canada and the United States agree on many social issues and questions of foreign policy, there are fundamental differences between them as well. A major break occurred in the

Canada and the United States dispute the ownership of fishing rights in these Pacific waters, where each country has occasionally seized the other's ships. At stake is the highly profitable salmon catch.

United States President Bill Clinton (R) laughs at something said by Canadian Prime Minister Jean Chretien during a joint news conference in Ottawa October 8, 1999. Chretien and Clinton spent the morning meeting before going onto Mont Tremblant, Quebec for the Conference on Federalism.

1960s and 1970s, when Canada did not support U.S. involvement in the Vietnam War. Approximately 25,000 young American men fled to Canada to escape the military draft. Canada has long been a haven for Americans who leave their country over matters of war or conscience. During the American Revolution, more than 40,000 colonists who remained loyal to Britain fled to Canada. During the 18th and 19th centuries, many American blacks escaping from slavery made their way into Canada along the Underground Railroad.

Despite their differences, the United States and Canada remain close allies and partners. And if Canada continues to gain economic power and international prestige, the proximity of the United States may become less overwhelming. For now, however, the feelings of many Canadians toward the United States may best be summed up in a remark by Pierre Trudeau, a former prime minister of Canada. He once told the U.S. Congress, "Living next to you is in some ways like sleeping with an elephant: No matter how friendly and even-tempered the beast, one is affected by every twitch and grunt."

Quebec and French Nationalism

In 1995, Quebec separatists narrowly lost a referendum to create a sovereign state. The vote was 50.6 percent to 49.4 percent to remain a Canadian province.

Quebec has long claimed to be a distinct society within Canada. About 80 percent of Quebec's population speak only French. They study in French schools and universities, work for companies that conduct business in French, and watch French television stations and movies made in French by French Canadian artists. Language is not Quebec's only distinctive feature, however. The province's political, legal, and social institutions differ from those found in the rest of Canada. Quebec is governed by a civil code that was developed from old French laws rather than from English common law as elsewhere in the nation, and its social programs have different rules and regulations than those of the other provinces.

For more than four centuries, the French-speaking people of Quebec have fought to retain their culture and language in a land where the vast majority of people have been English speakers of British descent. During the colonial era, this struggle between the

Opposite: French Canadians parade in the streets of Montreal on St. Jean Baptiste Day, June 25. The religious holiday is also a celebration of Quebec's nationalist spirit.
Above: Youthful demonstrators brandish Quebec's flag and call for the province to secede from Canada.

French explorer Jacques Cartier landed in Canada in 1534 and claimed the territory for France.

two factions was fought on the battlefield, as Britain and France strove for sovereignty over the New World colonies. Today, however, Quebec seeks to win recognition as a unique and distinct society within Canada through peaceful but direct political action—by amending Canada's constitution to give Quebec special rights and privileges, such as greater power to enact laws that affect immigration and language rights within the province, even though such laws might contradict the national constitution. Another recent attempt to amend the constitution and meet the demands of Quebec's French Canadians was the Meech Lake Accord, formulated by Prime Minister Brian Mulroney. This proposed constitutional amendment failed to become law in 1990 because two provinces—Manitoba and Newfoundland—refused to accept it. The failure of the Meech Lake Accord brought the Canadian nation to a crossroads. Quebec, a powerful political and economic entity, has threatened to separate from the nation if its demands are not met. But many English-speaking Canadians feel that the Québecois, the French-speaking people of Quebec, are already guaranteed sufficient privileges under the existing laws. Furthermore, some members of other ethnic groups resent the suggestion that French Canadian culture and language are more deserving of special attention than their own. Many Native Americans, in particular, feel that their political and economic rights have been abused to a much greater extent than those of the Québecois.

The question of Quebec's status in Canada is a complex and troubling issue with deep roots in the nation's history. The struggle between French and English speakers began in the mid-16th century, when European explorers first arrived in North America. In 1534, a 35-year-old Frenchman, explorer Jacques Cartier, became the first European to set foot in what is now Quebec. Planting a cross and the royal flag on the Gaspé Peninsula, he founded New France for King Francis I. The territory of New France eventually included much of what is now eastern Canada, the Mississippi Valley, and Louisiana. Britain took control of New France in 1763, but the importance of French colonization in the region remained evident in French family and place names and cultural traditions.

From the start, however, the British presence in the New World was stronger than the French. Significant French settlement in New France did not begin until 1608, when French explorer Samuel de Champlain built a fort at Quebec City from which fur traders and fishermen could operate. By 1628 the French colony had only 76 settlers, all of them at Champlain's fort. But by the same time the British had established several large colonies in present-day Canada and the United States. The British outnumbered the French in the New World by more than 20 to 1.

Between 1689 and 1763, Britain and France fought four major wars over the territory and resources of the New World. The final, decisive conflict was known as the Seven Years' War, and it ended in defeat for the French, who in 1763 signed the Treaty of Paris, surrendering almost all French territory in the New World to Britain. At this time Britain took control of Quebec.

Despite the pressures of the long war, the French colonists in Quebec had managed to develop a complex and close-knit society. They were unified by the French language, French civil law, and the Roman Catholic faith. All of these institutions set them apart from the English-speaking residents of the other colonies, most of whom were Protestants. Yet at first the French were treated rather well by their British conquerors. Hoping to make the French Canadians their allies against the rebellious colonists in what was to become the United States, the British passed the Quebec Act of 1774, which allowed French settlers to retain their language, religion, laws, customs, and land. But the British clearly retained political and economic power, especially since most of Quebec's political and business leaders had returned to France at the close of the Seven Years' War.

Fleeing the American Revolution, thousands of pro-British Loyalists from the American colonies arrived in Quebec, adding to the friction that had already been growing there between the English and the French. In 1791, Britain divided Quebec into two colonies, Upper Canada (now Ontario) for the English and Lower Canada (now Quebec) for the French. Although this act protected Quebec's religion and language, it did not change the fact that Britain controlled both colonies' economy and politics. Many

Samuel de Champlain founded the first important French settlements in New France. In 1608 he built a fort at the site of present-day Quebec City.

An 1893 painting by George Craig depicts the deportation of the Acadians, settlers of French ancestry who were driven from their Canadian homes in the mid-18th century when their territory fell under British control. Some Acadians managed to remain in the Atlantic provinces, where their culture survives today.

Québecois felt they had become second-class citizens in their own province, although they greatly outnumbered the English. French-speaking church leaders sometimes made the situation worse, protecting their own power and influence by siding with the British.

A series of violent revolts against the ruling elite began in 1837. A dynamic French lawyer named Louis-Joseph Papineau led the anti-British group. A skilled orator, he became the leader of the Parti Canadien (later Parti Patriote), which sought to wrest power from both the Roman Catholic church and the English-speaking business interests. Papineau's followers demanded the right to determine how the colony's funds were spent and sought control of its civil government. The rebellions were quickly crushed by British troops, but the sentiments of Papineau and his compatriots continued to echo in Quebec.

In 1867 the nation of Canada was created by the British North America Act. Four colonies—Canada East, Canada West, New Brunswick, and Nova Scotia—were united to form the Dominion of Canada. Canada East, which had a population of about 1.2 million, took back its original name of Quebec. Under the BNA, Quebec had two official languages, French and English. The act also gave the province direct control over education and civil law. The French Canadians of Quebec were partly satisfied by these guarantees, but tensions persisted between the English Canadians and the French Canadians. Quebec was a poor province that relied on Canada's newly created federal government for most of its revenue. Few of its abundant natural resources were being exploited; farming was at subsistence level, and the few French Canadian companies that existed were quite small. Opportunity seemed limited. Between 1850 and 1900, more than 500,000 Québecois left the province for the United States or western Canada.

Then, during the first half of the 20th century, Quebec gradually entered the Industrial Age and began to gain economic and political power. It did so largely on its own, without much help from the federal government. Determined to retain its distinctive social and cultural characteristics, Quebec rejected money that was offered by the federal government. As a result, Quebec's economy, educational system, and social institutions lagged far behind those of the rest of the nation until the 1960s.

The Not-So-Quiet Revolution

During the 1960s, Quebec took a large leap forward that came to be called the Quiet Revolution. This period brought a thorough overhauling of Quebec's economic, educational, and governmental systems. Economists were hired to devise a comprehensive economic plan. The administration of the schools was taken away from the church, and greater emphasis was placed on science and technical subjects. Social needs became a government concern, and health and unemployment insurance plans were enacted. The government expanded: Four new departments were created, including two to deal with educational and cultural matters.

With these gains came increased pressure from French Canadians for more political power on the national level, especially with regard to language and cultural rights. In 1963, Canada's federal government initiated an inquiry into the rights of French Canadians. Called the Royal Commission on Bilingualism and Biculturalism, this eight-year investigation concluded that French Canadians did not have the same rights and privileges as English

Canadians in business, education, and federal agencies. The study culminated in the 1969 Official Languages Act, which declared French and English to be the two official languages of Canada, not just of Quebec, and demanded that all federal institutions throughout the nation provide their services in both languages.

The year that the Royal Commission began its work saw the emergence of a new political movement in Quebec. The Front de Libération du Quebec (FLQ) was a violent revolutionary movement that favored the creation of an independent, French-speaking, socialist nation of Quebec. Throughout the 1960s, the FLQ used terrorist tactics, such as bombings and kidnappings, to promote this cause. But the FLQ was not the only group that wanted Quebec to separate from Canada, although it was the most violent and visible of the separatist organizations. A separatist party was created in 1968 by former members of the mainstream Liberal party. Called the Parti Québecois and led by René Lévesque, it supported what was known as sovereignty-association with the federal government, a plan that would have given Quebec far greater independence in provincial and even international politics while retaining a close economic association with Canada.

In 1970 the FLQ kidnapped and murdered Pierre Laporte, a Québecois politician. Fearful that the incident might cause rioting or other unrest, the federal government declared martial law and sent federal troops to Quebec. Hundreds of citizens were arrested and held without trial. Although most French Canadians were solidly against the FLQ's violence, this crisis polarized Quebec society. Many people felt compelled to adopt one of two extreme positions, either federalism or separatism.

The Parti Québecois was elected into power in the province in 1976. One of the first acts of the new government was the passage of Bill 101, which made French the sole official language in education, commerce, and public life. All public signs, it decreed, must be in French only. Bill 101 also required newly arrived immigrants to be schooled in French—not English—if they wanted to remain in Quebec.

In 1980, the Parti Québecois called for a referendum—a provincewide vote—on the question that had consumed the

Québecois for decades: Should Quebec separate from the rest of Canada and become a largely independent political unit? Canada's prime minister at the time was a Québecois named Pierre Trudeau. He wanted to keep Quebec in the Dominion of Canada, and he promised that if the people of Quebec voted no in the referendum the federal government would support a constitutional amendment giving special rights and privileges to Quebec. With this guarantee, the people of Quebec voted no, and Quebec remained part of the Canadian nation.

A new constitution was created for Canada in 1982, but it did not satisfy all of Quebec's demands. The Canadian Charter of Rights and Freedoms, which is part of the constitution, guarantees French-speaking Canadians *equal* rights and privileges by requiring both languages to be used in government and all official institutions, but it does not recognize Quebec as a distinct society worthy of *special* rights and privileges. As a result, Quebec did not accept the Constitution Act. The federal government faced the challenge of framing an amendment to the constitution

Federal troops in the streets of Montreal. The government invoked martial law after proindependence terrorists kidnapped several people in 1970. The incident ignited strong feelings on both sides of the independence question.

René Lévesque, shown at a rally in 1973, was a pivotal figure in the growth of Quebec's separatist movement. He founded the Parti Québecois in 1968 and became premier of the province in 1976.

that would satisfy Quebec's demands. Only then would Quebec accept the constitution, thus making a commitment to remain within the Dominion.

In early 1987 the premiers of Canada's 10 provinces met at Meech Lake, Quebec. Their goal was to devise an accord, or agreement, that would win Quebec's approval. The document they produced was called the Meech Lake Accord, and it would have given Quebec special rights—including the right to enact laws that might contradict the constitution—because of Quebec's special status as a unique French-speaking society within Canada. In order to become law, the Meech Lake Accord had to be agreed upon by all 10 provinces by June 1990.

For more than three years, the Meech Lake Accord and its consequences for Quebec and the Canadian nation dominated Canadian political life. But when the deadline came, two provinces had failed to accept the accord. The Native American population in Manitoba, acting on behalf of all Canadian Natives, refused to acknowledge Quebec as a distinct and special society until their own equally distinct heritage received the same recognition. Newfoundland rejected the Meech Lake Accord for reasons rooted in long-standing federal-provincial tensions. The premier of Newfoundland, Clyde Wells, felt that Prime Minister Brian Mulroney was putting too much pressure on the provinces to accept the accord, and he refused to permit a crucial vote that would have extended the deadline.

In the end, the Meech Lake Accord, which was meant to bring harmony to the discordant relations between French Canadians and English Canadians, produced only more discord. Dissappointed Quebec politicians formed a federal party, the Bloc Quebecois, to take their province out of Canada, and Brian Mulroney's Progressive Conservatives sought to halt the break-up of the country. He brokered a new agreement, the Charlottetown Accord of 1992, which included many of the elements of the failed Meech Lake agreement, but also new points. To satisfy westerners the Charlottetown Accord promised an elected, equal and effective Senate (much like the American House), and to satisfy Natives there was a promise to negotiate self-government. In October 1992 a countrywide vote was held and the Charlottetown Accord also failed to become law. Three years later the Quebec provincial government held another referendum on sovereignty association. Separatists lost the 1995 referendum by just 53,000 votes, out of 4.6 million cast. While French has become the second official language of Canada, the desire for independence lingers.

Native Peoples and Native Issues

During what has become known as the Indian Summer of 1990, Canada's Native Americans achieved a long-standing goal: They focused the attention of the country's white majority on the political and economic plight of the Native population. For the first time, the needs and concerns of Native Americans became more than a passing concern for local authorities. Native issues were front-page news across the nation in two separate and highly controversial incidents.

At the end of June, Elijah Harper, a legislator from the province of Manitoba who is a member of the Cree Nation, played a central role in the defeat of the Meech Lake Accord, a proposed amendment to Canada's constitution that would have given the province of Quebec special recognition as a "distinct society" because of its French heritage. Speaking for Natives throughout Canada, Harper refused to acknowledge Quebec's special status, claiming that the Native peoples of Canada deserved the same recognition. Harper's opposition was a decisive blow to the Meech Lake Accord, for without the support of all provinces, it could not become law.

Opposite: In the summer of 1990, Canadian military personnel approach masked Mohawk protesters to discuss the removal of barricades that the Quebec Natives had built across a nearby road. The confrontation between Native groups and the federal government exploded into violence that summer.
Above: Mohawk spokesmen Thomas Porter, Mike Mitchell, and Harold Tarbell (left to right) are among those who are trying to gain a wider hearing for Native views in Canada.

Elijah Harper, a Cree legislator from Manitoba, focused attention on Native complaints when he blocked an amendment to Canada's constitution that would have given Quebec's French-speaking society special status within the country.

A few weeks later, Native Canadians once again made national and international headlines, when a long-simmering dispute over land ownership in Quebec erupted into violence. A group of Quebec's Mohawk placed barricades across a road near the town of Oka, about 19 miles (30 kilometers) west of Montreal. The Mohawk wanted to halt the town's plan to extend a local golf course onto land claimed by the Mohawk. After lengthy negotiations failed to resolve the issue, the Quebec government sent a police tactical force to bring down the barricade. About 100 police used assault rifles, concussion grenades, and tear gas on the Mohawk protesters, who retaliated during a three-hour melee in which a policeman was shot to death. The government finally forced the Mohawk to surrender, and several hundred Mohawks faced criminal charges.

These controversies reflect the two main goals of Canada's Native Americans: to achieve increased political power on the national level, and to regain control of their traditional lands. The part of the government with which the Natives most often interact is the Department of Indian Affairs and Northern Development (DIAND), a federal agency in charge of Native issues. DIAND oversees the administration of the Indian Act, first enacted in 1876 and later amended, which regulates the status of Canada's Natives.

The struggle for Native rights is a growing issue throughout Canada. Various Native peoples lived in what is now Canada for thousands of years before the first Europeans arrived. Many Natives feel that the land where Canadians have built cities, drilled for oil, and cultivated farms was unfairly taken from its original inhabitants. Furthermore, once displaced, the Natives were treated as second-class citizens, forced to live on reserves, denied the right to speak their languages and practice traditional customs, and not allowed to vote. Although the laws have since been changed to guarantee the Natives' civil rights, Native communities still lag behind white communities by many social and economic standards. Natives today have the highest unemployment rate in Canada—higher than 17 percent on the reserves, more than twice the national average. The percentage of

Natives who receive college degrees is less than half that of the general population. Life expectancy for most Native groups is about 10 years less than the national average, and the suicide rate of Natives is nearly 3 times that of the general population.

By all indications, however, conditions for most Native groups have been improving over the last few decades. At least some of this progress can be related to the activism of Native rights organizations. Chief among these organizations is the Assembly of First Nations (AFN), which has concentrated on trying to obtain constitutional support for greater Native self-government. Canada's Native population has become much more urban over the past two decades. More than half now live in urban settings while 30% live in major cities.

The Native Population

Canada's constitution recognizes three types of Natives. These are the Métis, people of mixed Native and European heritage; the Inuit, a group of peoples in the far north who are more closely

A Native reserve in the 1960s. Living conditions for the Natives still lag far behind those of most Canadians.

A Native of central Canada, photographed in 1907

related to the northern peoples of Asia and Europe than to other Canadian Natives; and the North American Indians, consisting of many cultural and tribal groups who have traditionally inhabited non-Arctic Canada. Anthropologists classify the Natives another way—by the languages they speak. Canada has 11 large families of Native languages: Algonquian, Iroquoian, Siouan, Athapaskan, Kootenayan, Salishan, Wakashan, Tsimshian, Haida, Tlingit, and Inuktitut.

According to the 1996 census, Natives make up about 3 percent of the total population, or about 799,010 people. Most Natives live in western and northern Canada. About 59 percent of the population in the Northwest Territories and 21 percent of the population in the Yukon Territory claim Native ancestry. About 8 percent of Manitobans and Saskatchewanians are Native.

About 550,000 Canadians claimed in the 1996 census to have at least some North American Indian ancestry. More than 62 percent of these 550,000 are considered "status Indians"—those who can prove a blood relationship to one of the 595 Indian groups that were registered under the original Indian Act and assigned land reserves. Status Indians are eligible for a number of benefits, including free education after high school and exemption from federal and some provincial income and sales taxes. About 62 percent of Canada's North American Indians live on approximately 2,251 reserves covering 6.4 million acres (2.6 million hectares) across the country. Of the Indians who do not live on the reserves, most live in cities, especially Toronto, Montreal, Winnipeg, and Vancouver.

Métis number about 210,190 according to the 1996 census, but the actual number is unknown because the term Métis is not clearly defined. Some people consider any person with mixed Indian and European blood to be a Métis. Others believe that the term refers only to those whose ancestors were of Indian and French ancestry from one of the prairie provinces (Saskatchewan, Manitoba, or Alberta).

The Métis of Manitoba and Saskatchewan are well-represented in Canadian history. Seeking self-government, they battled the Canadian government in two uprisings in the late 19th century. Their leader, Louis Riel, was executed for treason but is now regarded by some Canadians as a heroic freedom fighter. Later, the Métis of Alberta organized and lobbied for political rights, some of which were granted under the Métis Betterment Act of 1938. The Métis were not included in the original Indian Act and do not have the same status as the North American Indians, but Métis political activity has intensified since the mid-1960s. A number of local and regional political organizations, including the Manitoba Métis Federation, the Ontario Métis Association, and the Louis Riel Association of British Columbia, are active. On the national level, the Métis are represented by the Native Council of Canada and the Métis National Council.

The Inuit number about 100,000 worldwide. More than 27,000 of them live in Canada; the rest live in Alaska and Greenland. The Inuit of Canada are divided into eight tribal

A Native fisherman spears salmon in a stream in British Columbia. The traditional way of life of many of Canada's Pacific coast Native peoples revolves around salmon fishing.

groups: the Ungava, Labrador, Baffinland, Igulik, Caribou, Netsilik, Copper, and Western Arctic Inuit. Most of them live in small communities in the Northwest Territories and in northern Quebec and Newfoundland. Most Inuit communities are located on bays, inlets, or river mouths, reflecting a culture that has traditionally revolved around fishing and hunting in Arctic waters.

The Inuit have never been subject to the Indian Act, although they and their lands have been under federal control since 1939. The Inuit Tapirisat of Canada, a Native rights group, was founded in 1971 to represent the Inuit in discussions of such issues as the economic development of the Canadian north and the preservation of Inuit culture.

Native Peoples and the Law

Early legal relations between Natives and Europeans were often concerned with trade. Before confederation in 1867, such agreements were made in the colonies of Upper Canada, Lower Canada, Nova Scotia, New Brunswick, Prince Edward Island, and British Columbia. The British North America Act of 1867, which created the Dominion of Canada, gave Canada's Parliament jurisdiction over "Indians and lands reserved for Indians."

In 1876, Parliament passed the Indian Act. One goal of this act was to force the Natives to give up their traditions and ways of life in favor of European customs and culture. This was called enfranchisement and was the cornerstone of Canadian Native policy throughout much of the country's history. By enfranchising, a Native supposedly consented to abandon his or her Native identity and community in order to merge with the non-Native majority. Traditional Native ceremonies and practices were officially suppressed under the Indian Act.

Certain rules and regulations under the Indian Act and other laws forced some Natives into the category of nonstatus Indian. For example, a Native woman who married a non-Native man lost her Indian status, as did her children. Men could lose Indian status by joining the Canadian armed forces. The loss of Indian

A Native family near White-horse in the Yukon Territory. Natives make up a larger share of the total population in Canada's two northern territories than anywhere else in the country.

status could be a great hardship, because individuals who lost it were no longer eligible for the government support that was given to status Indians on reserved lands.

Pressure by Native groups led to significant changes in the Indian Act in 1985. The changes brought a substantial increase in the number of status Indians in Canada, as those who had lost Indian status through marriage were permitted to rejoin their bands as official members; an unfortunate side effect of this new change, however, was added pressure on the funds and resources of some Native bands. Another change in the Indian Act gave the Natives greater powers to regulate the economic and political organization of the reserves, although the scope of these powers is yet unclear.

Canadian Natives gather on Parliament Hill in Ottawa to protest the Hydro-Quebec project that created reservoirs and power stations on Cree land in the early 1970s.

Since 1973, the federal government and various Native groups representing the Indians, Inuit, and Métis have been trying to settle two broad categories of Native land claims—comprehensive and specific. Comprehensive claims are based on continued traditional Native use and occupancy of lands and waters that are not covered by any previous treaty. Specific claims are based on grievances that Native people have about the fulfillment—or lack of fulfillment—of existing treaties or other formal agreements.

One of the most earnest land claim struggles now under way in Canada pits the Cree people of Quebec's James Bay region against Hydro-Quebec, one of the most powerful energy companies in North America, which is owned by the province of Quebec. In the 1970s, Hydro-Quebec negotiated a settlement with the Cree that allowed the company to build a series of reservoirs, some of which were 60 miles across and 30 miles wide (96 kilometers by 48 kilometers), and a vast system of power stations to provide electricity for use in Quebec and for sale to the United States. Before the project was completed, more than 220,000 square miles (569,800 square kilometers) of Cree territory was flooded or developed.

As compensation, the Cree were paid a large sum of money and some were relocated to a modern village built by the government of Quebec. But their traditional way of life—fishing and hunting in the bush—was changed forever. In addition, the environment has been gravely damaged by chemical pollution; mercury levels in fish are so high that the Cree have been warned not to fish in certain areas.

In 1993, the Cree signed a $50 million compensation package with Hydro-Quebec for social, economic and environmental losses from the first phase of the La Grande Hydro project. A project to expand operations in northern Quebec by damming the Great Whale River near Hudson Bay was shelved in 1994 due to environmental and media pressures brought by the Cree. The Cree of the Great Whale region strongly oppose the new project and have vowed to fight it. One Cree leader, Dennis Bearskin, told a reporter for the *Boston Globe,* "We got money for our land. But that was nothing. To the Cree, the land is more important."

Most recently the Nisga'a of British Columbia were awarded some 2000 square kilometers of territory, about $200 million dollars, extensive logging and fishing rights, and a large measure of self-government. As of May 2000 the Nisga'a are no longer under the federal Indian Act and in some cases their local laws will override federal and provincial regulations. In return the Nisga'a have agreed to begin paying sales and income tax over the next decade. Many Natives in Canada, who remember the strained relations of that "Indian Summer" of 1990, hope the Nisga'a treaty is only the first in a long line of agreements offering more control over their land and ways of life.

The Canadian People

According to official 1999 estimates, about 30,491,300 people live in Canada's 3,851,790 square miles (9,978,653 square kilometers). Canada's population density—about 7 people per square mile (3 per square kilometer)—is one of the lowest among modern nations. Although Canada is the second largest country in the world in area (after Russia), it ranks 31st in population.

About 80 percent of Canadians live within 200 miles (320 kilometers) of Canada's border with the United States. More than 62 percent of Canadians live in the provinces of Quebec and Ontario. Much of the rest of Canada, with its rugged terrain and severe climate, is uninhabited or thinly populated. Only Ontario, Alberta, British Columbia, and the Northwest Territories have experienced gains in population in recent years; the other seven provinces and the Yukon Territory have steadily decreasing populations.

The majority of Canadians are city dwellers, living in one of the 23 metropolitan areas that have populations of more than

Opposite: Saskatchewan's Qu'Appelle River valley produces potatoes, vegetables, and grain crops. The farms of Canada are among the world's most productive, although only five percent of Canadians are farmers. *Above:* The Trade and Convention Centre in Vancouver, one of the country's fastest-growing cities.

Native artifacts such as this Haida mask from British Columbia are increasingly recognized as a precious and distinctive part of Canada's artistic heritage.

100,000 people. The 3 largest cities are Montreal, Quebec (population 1,016,376); Toronto, Ontario (population 653,734); and Winnipeg, Manitoba (population 618,477). Urbanites enjoy a wide range of cultural amenities, including first-class museums, libraries, symphonies, dance companies, theaters, and restaurants.

In spite of rapid growth during the second half of the 20th century, most Canadian cities have managed to avoid the high crime rates that plague many American and European cities. But homelessness, especially in Toronto and Vancouver, has proved to be a growing problem.

Canada was once a rural nation, but now only one-fifth of all Canadians live in the country. Of this number, about 5 percent are farmers, mostly in the prairie provinces of Alberta, Manitoba, and Saskatchewan, which contain more than 75 percent of Canada's farmland. Other rural occupations include logging, mining, and fishing. An increasing number of country dwellers commute to major towns or cities to work.

Canada's Cultural Mosaic

According to the 1996 census, recent immigrants account for about 16.1 percent of Canada's population, and the percentage of immigrants grows every year. From 1991–1996, 1,038,990 new immigrants arrived from other shores to live in Canada. Immigration is overseen by a federal agency called the Canada Employment and Immigration Commission (CEIC).

When the Europeans first arrived in what is today Canada, the land was already inhabited by approximately 220,000 Native Americans. For nearly three centuries, the population of Native groups rapidly declined. Since the 1940s, however, the Native population has increased. About 711,000 people, or 3 percent of the total population, claim at least 1 Native parent.

For 200 years after Jacques Cartier landed in Quebec in 1534, most settlers were French. Many settled in Quebec, which is still distinctively French; others settled in the region called Acadia, consisting of Prince Edward Island, Nova Scotia, New Brunswick, and part of Newfoundland. Then a flood of people of British origin began to arrive from England, Scotland, Ireland, and later the United States. People whose heritage is either French or British still make up the majority of the population, and English and French are Canada's two official languages. Since the late 19th century, however, immigration from other European countries and from Asia, the Caribbean, and Africa has increased. Of all Canadians who report having neither British nor French ancestry, more than half are of European descent. But since the 1970s, Asian immigration has been on the rise, particularly in British Columbia. Many Chinese from Hong Kong emigrated to Canada to avoid becoming part of the People's Republic of China when Hong Kong joined that nation in 1997; other Asian immigrants include Vietnamese, Laotian, and Cambodian refugees.

Each part of Canada has a distinctive ethnic composition. Newfoundland has the most homogenous population—that is, the highest percentage of people with the same ethnic background: More than 80 percent of its population is of British descent. In Quebec, 78 percent of the people are French. Blacks make up about 3 percent of the nation's total population, and most of them are concentrated in Ontario, although there has been a black population in Nova Scotia since the 18th century, and race riots in Halifax, Nova Scotia, have made headlines during the 1980s and 1990s. The population is more diverse in the western provinces. The Northwest Territories is the only part of the country where neither British nor French is the largest group; more than 52 percent of people in the Northwest Territories are Natives.

Today—from the Scottish of Nova Scotia to the Ukrainians of Saskatchewan to the Japanese of British Columbia—Canada's people form an ethnic mosaic that stretches from sea to sea. Encouraged by official government policy to keep their cultural traditions alive, immigrant groups retain their heritages, including traditional names, languages, religions, cuisines, and customs, while at the same time adjusting to Canadian ways of life.

The West Wind, painted in 1917, is one of the best-known works by Ontario artist Tom Thomson.

Canada's policy of encouraging ethnic identity is overseen by the Multiculturalism Directorate of the Department of the Secretary of State, established in 1973. The directorate sponsors cultural education and arts programs in schools, libraries, and museums throughout the country. One result of Canada's emphasis on multiculturalism is its abundance of ethnic festivals, ranging from the Acadian Festival in Prince Edward Island to the Kamloops Indian Band Pow Wow Days in British Columbia. Canadians are encouraged to celebrate and enjoy the contributions made to their history and culture by each ethnic group. Yet some Canadians complain that the government's emphasis on cultural support for ethnic minorities helps mask the fact that certain minorities have little or no political or economic power.

Creating a National Culture

At first influenced by European traditions, later overwhelmed by popular culture from the United States, Canadian artists and writers have long struggled to develop their own specifically Canadian style and identity. The first artists to be seen as distinctly Canadian were a cluster of painters called the Group of Seven. Formed during the 1910s, the Group of Seven included Tom Thomson, A. Y. Jackson, and Lawren Harris. These artists helped define a Canadian style by looking with fresh eyes at Canada's impressive landscapes. Reviewing a Group of Seven exhibition, one critic wrote, "Canada reveals herself in colors all her own. . . . We feel the rush of mighty winds . . . the swirl and roar of the swollen river torrents, and the awful silent majesty of her snows."

Each of Canada's regions, from the rocky coasts of the Atlantic to the rolling wheat fields of the central prairies to the mountains and rainforests of the west, has produced its share of artists and writers. The late Margaret Laurence, one of Canada's most popular English-language writers, set her novels in small Manitoba farming villages. French-Canadian author Gabrielle Roy has described the lives of working-class people of Montreal in her fiction. Quebec's thriving French Canadian film industry draws inspiration from both the urban sprawl of Montreal and the vast northern tundra. And the Inuit arts of the north, including sculpture and storytelling, are receiving increased attention around the world.

Because of its proximity, the United States has an enormous influence on Canadian life. In many ways, the nearness of American culture has made it difficult for Canadians to develop a national culture of their own. The most popular magazines in Canada—*Time, Newsweek,* and *People*—are published in the United States. When Canadians watch television or go to the movies, they are very likely to watch shows and films produced in Hollywood. In pop music, fashion, and the fine arts, Americans have usually led the way and saturated the marketplace.

Although most Canadians enjoy and admire American culture, many also resent its prominence in their country. In the

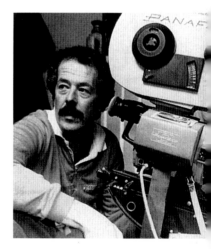

French Canadian Denys Arcand is one of Canada's most acclaimed contemporary filmmakers. His movies include *Jesus of Montreal* and *The Decline of the American Empire.*

1930s the Canadian government began establishing national institutions to help foster Canadian culture, and government support for home-grown arts continues: Funding for the arts amounted to nearly $5 billion, about 1.6 percent of total spending, in 1988.

The Canadian Broadcasting Corporation (CBC) was created by Parliament in 1936 to "foster a national spirit and interpret national citizenship." Today, the CBC provides national, regional, and local radio and television programs in both French and English. It also broadcasts locally produced programs in English and Native languages to the far north; runs a multilingual shortwave service for listeners overseas; and provides closed captioning for the deaf. About 78 percent of the CBC's television programs and 80 percent of its radio shows are produced by Canadians.

The 1930s gave birth to another important public institution, the National Film Board of Canada (NFB). Since 1939, documentaries, features, and short films produced with the support of the NFB have won hundreds of awards. The Canadian Film Development Corporation and Telefilm Canada are two other government organizations that help promote Canada's film industry.

One of the most important national arts institutions is the Canada Council, an independent agency created by Parliament in 1957. The Council provides about 4,500 grants and services each year to professional Canadian artists and organizations in dance, media, music, opera, theater, publishing, and the visual arts. Add in the 11,151 payments to authors through the Public Lending Right Commission and the Council, in 1999, awarded a total of $102 million.

Opened in 1969 and financed in part by the federal government, the National Arts Centre in Ottawa is a multidisciplinary, bilingual performing arts center. Performances of its touring dance, theater, and music companies and broadcasts of its performances in French and English reach a total audience of about 700,000 each year.

During the 1960s, the federal government tried to enhance and expand the country's national museums. Four national museums are found in the Ottawa–Hull region. They are the National

An orchestral performance in Toronto

Hockey is the country's national winter sport—and the favorite activity of many young Canadians. Lacrosse is Canada's national summer sport.

Gallery of Canada, a fine arts museum; the Canadian Museum of Nature, a natural history collection; the National Museum of Science and Technology, which features hands-on exhibits and displays of scientific discoveries and advances; and the Canadian Museum of Civilization, which collects, preserves, and displays artifacts from Canada's cultural heritage. In 1989, a spectacular new building for this museum opened, featuring galleries for Native crafts and folk arts and traditions, as well as a theater using the latest film technology.

In addition to their multicultural heritage and arts institutions, Canadians are unified by another powerful force: the national pastime of hockey. By far the most popular sport in the nation, hockey was invented in Canada in the late 19th century. Since the founding of the National Hockey League (NHL) in 1909, Canadian athletes have dominated the sport, attracting millions of avid fans throughout Canada and the United States. Such stars as Wayne Gretzky, Maurice Richard, Gordie Howe, and Guy Lafleur have become national heroes, reflecting the Canadian spirit in their energy, talent, and national pride.

Further Reading

Armitage, Peter. *The Innu.* New York: Chelsea House, 1990.

Berton, Pierre. *The Arctic Grail: The Quest for the Northwest Passage and the North Pole.* New York: Viking Penguin, 1988.

———. *Drifting Home.* New York: Knopf, 1974.

———. *Flames Across the Border: 1814.* Toronto: McClelland and Stewart, 1981.

———. *The Impossible Railway: The Building of the Canadian Pacific.* New York: Knopf, 1974.

———. *The Invasion of Canada: 1812–13.* Toronto: McClelland and Stewart, 1980.

Creighton, Donald. *Canada's First Century: 1867–1967.* New York: St. Martin's Press, 1970.

Fingard, Judith. *Jack in Port: Sailortowns of Eastern Canada.* Toronto: University of Toronto Press, 1982.

Francis, R. D., Richard Jones, and D. B. Smith. *Destinies: Canadian History Since Confederation.* Toronto: Holt, Rinehart & Winston, 1988.

———. *Origins: Canadian History to Confederation.* Toronto: Holt, Rinehart & Winston, 1988.

Frideres, James. *Canada's Indians: Contemporary Conflicts.* Englewood Cliffs, NJ: Prentice-Hall, 1974.

Hocking, Anthony. *The Yukon and the Northwest Territories.* New York: McGraw-Hill Ryerson, 1979.

Holbrook, Sabra. *Canada's Kids.* New York: Atheneum, 1983.

Law, Kevin. *Canada.* New York: Chelsea House, 1990.

Lévesque, René. *Memoirs.* Toronto: McClelland and Stewart, 1986.

Malcolm, Andrew. *The Canadians.* New York: Random House, 1985.

Manore, Jean. *Cross-Currents: Hydroelectricity and the Engineering of Northern Ontario.* Wilfrid Laurier University Press, 1999.

McNaught, Kenneth. *The Penguin History of Canada.* New York: Penguin Books, 1988.

Miller, J. R. *Skyscrapers Hide the Heavens: A History of Indian-White Relations in Canada. Toronto:* University of Toronto Press, 1989.

Moore, Christopher. *1867: How the Fathers Made a Deal.* McClelland & Stewart, 1998.

Newman, Peter C. *Caesars of the Wilderness: The Story of the Hudson's Bay Company,* vol. II. New York: Penguin Books, 1988.

————. *A Company of Adventurers: The Story of the Hudson's Bay Company,* vol. I. New York: Penguin Books, 1985.

Perkins, Jack. *Acadia: Visions and Verse.* Down East Books, 1999.

Scott, J. M. *Icebound: Journeys to the Northwest Sea.* London: Gordon and Cremonesi, 1977.

Shephard, Jennifer. *Canada.* Chicago: Childrens Press, 1987.

Smith, P. J., ed. *The Prairie Provinces.* Toronto: University of Toronto Press, 1972.

Statistics Canada. *Canada: A Portrait.* Ottawa: Statistics Canada, 1991.

Taner, Ogden. *The Canadians.* New York: Time-Life Books, 1977.

Wansbrough, M. B. *Great Canadian Lives.* New York: Doubleday, 1986.

Webb, Melody. *The Last Frontier.* Albuquerque: University of New Mexico Press, 1985.

Woodcock, George. *The Canadians.* Cambridge: Harvard University Press, 1979.

————. *The Hudson's Bay Company.* New York: Macmillan, 1970.

————. *A Picture History of British Columbia.* Seattle: University of Washington Press, 1982.

Index

ACKNOWLEDGMENTS
Courtesy of Art Gallery of Ontario/gift of the Canadian Club, Toronto: p. 54;
The Bettmann Archive: p. 32; Diana Blume: p. 6; Canadian Consulate: pp. 5,
15, 27, 50, 51, 52, 57; Courtesy of Canadian International Development
Agency: p. 26; Courtesy of Canadian National Defense Headquarters: p. 22;
Canadian Pacific Corporate Archives: p. 18; Canapress Photo Service: p. 55;
Courtesy of Department of Library Services, American Museum of Natural
History: p. 13 (neg. # 19311); Hudson's Bay Company Archives/Provincial
Archives of Manitoba: p. 14; Image West Photography: p. 28; Courtesy of
Indian and Northern Affairs Canada: pp. 45, 47; Industry, Science and
Technology of Canada: pp. 3, 12, 56; Lawrence/DND/Courtesy of National
Archives of Canada: p. 24 (neg. # PA-133246); Library of Congress: p. 33;
Courtesy of Musée Acadien, Université de Moncton, photo by Léo Blanchard:
p. 34; Courtesy of National Archives of Canada: pp. 19 (neg. # C-56088), 43
(neg. # PA119742); Provincial Archives of Manitoba/Edmund Morris
Collection: p. 44; Reuters/Bettmann Archive: pp. 23, 29, 30, 31, 40, 42;
G. P. Roberts/Public Archives of Canada/C-733: p. 17; UPI/Bettmann Archive:
pp. 37, 38, 41, 48; Reuters/Archive Photo: p. 20

Suzanne LeVert has contributed several volumes to Chelsea House's CANADA IN THE 21ST CENTURY series. She is the author of four previous books for young readers. One of these, *The Sakharov File,* a biography of noted Russian physicist Andrei Sakharov, was selected as a Notable Book by the National Council for the Social Studies. Her other books include *AIDS: In Search of a Killer, The Doubleday Book of Famous Americans,* and *New York.* Ms. LeVert also has extensive experience as an editor, first in children's books at Simon & Schuster, then as associate editor at *Trialogue,* the magazine of the Trilateral Commission, and as senior editor at Save the Children, the international relief and development organization. She lives in Cambridge, Massachusetts.

George Sheppard, General Editor, is an instructor at Upper Canada College in Toronto. Dr. Sheppard earned his Ph.D. in Canadian History at McMaster University in Hamilton, Ontario and has taught at McMaster, Laurentian, and Nipissing Universities. His research specialty is Canadian Social History and he has published items in *Histoire sociale/Social History, The Canadian Historical Review, The Beaver, Canadian Social Studies, The Annual Bulletin of Historical Literature, Canadian Military History, The Historical Dictionary of the British Empire, The Encyclopedia of POW's and the Internment,* and *The Dictionary of Canadian Biography.* He has also worked as a historical consultant for educational material in both multimedia and print format and has published a book entitled *Plunder, Profit and Paroles: A Social History of the War of 1812 in Upper Canada.* Dr. Sheppard is a native of Timmins, Ontario.

Pierre Berton, Senior Consulting Editor, is the author of 34 books, including *The Mysterious North, Klondike, Great Canadians, The Last Spike, The Great Railway Illustrated, Hollywood's Canada, My Country: The Remarkable Past, The Wild Frontier, The Invasion of Canada, Why We Act Like Canadians, The Klondike Quest,* and *The Arctic Grail.* He has won three Governor General's Awards for creative nonfiction, two National Newspaper Awards, and two ACTRA "Nellies" for broadcasting. He is a Companion of the Order of Canada, a member of the Canadian News Hall of Fame, and holds 12 honorary degrees. Raised in the Yukon, Mr. Berton began his newspaper career in Vancouver. He then became managing editor of *McLean's,* Canada's largest magazine, and subsequently worked for the Canadian Broadcasting Network and the *Toronto Star.* He lives in Kleinburg, Ontario.